Have You Met Jesus?

**Eight Studies
On The Life And Times
Of Jesus**

E. Dale Click

CSS Publishing Company, Inc., Lima, Ohio

HAVE YOU MET JESUS?

Copyright © 1997 by
CSS Publishing Company, Inc.
Lima, Ohio

All rights reserved. No part of this publication may be reproduced in any manner whatsoever without the prior permission of the publisher, except in the case of brief quotations embodied in critical articles and reviews. Inquiries should be addressed to: Permissions, CSS Publishing Company, Inc., P.O. Box 4503, Lima, Ohio 45802-4503.

Some quotations are from the *New Revised Standard Version of the Bible*, copyright 1989 by the Division of Christian Education of the National Council of the Churches of Christ in the USA. Used by permission.

Some quotations are from the *King James Version of the Bible*, in the public domain.

Library of Congress Cataloging-in-Publication Data

Click, E. Dale.
   Have you met Jesus? : eight studies on his life and times / E. Dale Click.
     p.   cm.
   ISBN 0-7880-1016-6 (pbk.)
   1. Jesus Christ—Biography. I. Title.
BT301.2.C539   1996
232.9'01—dc21   96-44069
[B]   CIP

ISBN 0-7880-1016-6   PRINTED IN U.S.A

In memory of my beloved wife, Martha Jane Gray Click, who entered the Church Triumphant August 31, 1996. She reviewed this manuscript before her untimely death. She was a biblical scholar, faithful companion, and helper for 52 years.

Table of Contents

Introduction	7
1. Preparation For Ministry	9
2. Ministry Midst Obscurity	17
3. Ministry Midst Popularity	27
4. Ministry Midst Opposition	35
5. Ministry Midst Decision	43
6. Ministry Midst Determination	51
7. Ministry Midst Death	59
8. Fulfillment Of Prophecy	67

Introduction

In a small group discussion at a church I served three questions were asked: 1) If you were to describe the life of Jesus Christ, what would you say? 2) If you were talking with a person who had never heard of Jesus Christ, who would you say He is? 3) Have you ever met Jesus Christ?

The first question revealed the usual statements made about Jesus' birth at Bethlehem: a sojourn into Jerusalem when He was twelve years old; a few recollections about his miracles and parables; and his death on a cross. It was Sunday School memory time.

The second question prompted more insight. The identity of Christ became the focus of discussion. The meanings of familiar words were re-examined: shepherd, Savior, Lord, Master, Son of God, and so forth. But to explain to a person who had never heard of Jesus Christ just who He is became a thought provoking task. No one had Jesus' driver's license to pass around!

The third question prompted consternation and some self-defense. "What is meant by this question? You mean, in person?" "You mean I'm supposed to have some personal encounter with someone I can't see? Saint Paul, maybe, but not me!"

The evening discussion was enlightening to me. Implanted in my thoughts came the realization that many devoted church members needed not only to know more about their true God, Jesus Christ, but also to experience his presence. At the conclusion of the discussion someone said, "Maybe a series of sermons on Jesus would be helpful to believers and non-believers alike. How about it, Pastor?" I thought they would never ask! And that is how this series of messages on the life and times of Jesus Christ came about.

This series can be given on Sundays or Wednesdays in Lent, plus Holy Week, or scheduled as a summer series. I have tried giving them in Lent and summer. Either time, sustained interest occurred. Believers, and those who have not made a commitment to Christ, are eager to hear and learn more about this true God. May this series prompt others not to take for granted the public's knowledge of the life and times of Jesus, as I had!

— EDC, May, 1996

1. Preparation For Ministry

Scripture Reading: Luke 2:25-39

Prayer: Let us talk with God:
    "Jesus, the very thought of you
    Fills us with sweet delight;
    But sweeter far your face to view
    And rest within your light.
    No voice can sing, no heart can frame,
    Nor can the mind recall
    A sweeter sound than your blest name,
    O Savior of us all!"[1]

†   †   †

    The President of Peru, riding in his ancient carriage drawn by six white horses, escorted by a hundred or more soldiers in their shining armor riding on sleek, curried horses, passed the place in the city square of Lima where my camera was poised for action. Just then my camera jammed!

    At the climax of Jesus' life, He was led up a broad avenue, through a park laid out with walks, ponds, and trees, to the magnificent palace of Herod the Great where Pontius Pilate asked the question of the centuries: "... What should I do with Jesus who is called the Messiah?" (Matthew 27:22). Just at this climax of Lent is exactly when many a faith jams and fails to record the Savior who passes by. But, if your Lenten camera is focused and functioning, it will record the words of Simon Peter, "Lord, to whom can we go? You have the words of eternal life. We have come to believe and know that you are the Holy One of God" (John 6:68-69).

Get your Lenten camera set now for a panning of Jesus' life. In these eight worship celebrations, we shall try to frame a Person — the second Person of the Trinity.

Any camera which tries to catch the life of Jesus should first focus attention on the preparation He made for living the life He did.

He lived humbly. The little babe born in a stable grew up in a carpenter's home. He lived in a home of godly and hard working common folk. The very fact that Joseph, the head of the household, is not mentioned later in the life of Christ leads us to believe that Joseph died during the youth of Jesus. If so, Jesus experienced a death in the family, as many of us do. As the firstborn, he would have had to work hard and care for the household. There were four other sons and at least two sisters, according to Matthew (Matthew 13:55, 56). Two of the brothers, James and Jude, gave us epistles in the Bible.

Jesus must have received his education at home and from the scribe of the village synagogue. Hebrew was a natural study for him although it was a dead language, even in Palestine. His language was Aramaic, a branch of the same stem to which Hebrew belongs. It is very likely He learned Greek, too, although we have no evidence of it. Jesus, a multi-lingual person, was able to converse with the people of his land.

Jesus grew up in one of the most beautiful places in the world. Nazareth is situated in a secluded cup-like valley amid the mountains of Zebulon. There are white houses with vines clinging to their walls, gardens and groves of olive, fig, orange, and pomegranate trees. From the village of Nazareth, on a hill 500 feet high, you can see the mountains of Galilee. It was this village, his hometown, where later at the beginning of his ministry the townspeople tried to throw him off a cliff because He claimed to be the fulfillment of Scripture. From this vantage point you can see 9,232-foot snowcapped Mount Hermon towering above to the north. You can see the ridge of Carmel, a range of fertile, forested hills; the coast of Tyre, the leading city of Phoenicia, off the coast of southern Lebanon; the sparkling waters of the Mediterranean to the west; the wooded, cone-like bulk of 1,043-foot Tabor to the east; to the south the plain of Esdraelon, the western section of the valleys and plains that separate Galilee from Samaria; and the mountains of Ephraim beyond.

Jesus must have enjoyed the landscape and the sea. Sleeping on a boat, stretched out upon a bed of rushes or in a string hammock, wherever He had a place to rest and sleep, just as one of us, Jesus lived the human life.

Jesus noted the history and the times in which He lived. By the time of Jesus, David was a hero of history of some 1,000 years. Four hundred years had elapsed since the prophet Malachi. Since that time no great prophet had spoken for God. Many changes had taken place in Palestine. If Malachi or David or other prophets had returned on the scene in Jesus' time, they would not have recognized the language, the customs, the ideas, the political parties, or the institutions.

Politically, the country had changed hands several times, conqueror after conqueror marching over it. Finally, the country was completely under the mighty power of Rome. Rome divided it into several small sections. Galilee and Peraea were ruled by petty kings, sons of that Herod who ruled when Jesus was born and who had tried to kill him. Judea was under the charge of a Roman official, a subordinate of the governor of Syria, also a Roman province. Roman soldiers marched through the streets of Jerusalem. Roman symbols waved. Roman money was used. Roman tax collectors sat at the gate of every town.

The Sanhedrin, the supreme Jewish body of government, was reduced to a shadow of its power. Its presidents, the high priests, were mere puppets of Rome.

In religion, the changes had been equally great. In external appearance, it may have sounded like progress, much like some think of religion in our day. Yes, the country was more orthodox. Idolatry had been banished. The priestly orders had been reorganized. Temple services and annual feasts were observed with strict regularity. A new and very important religious institution developed — the synagogue with its rabbis. Every Sabbath the synagogues were filled with praying congregations. Sermons were delivered by the rabbis. The language of Hebrew was reintroduced.

The Hebrew Scriptures, our Old Testament, were reread once a year. Schools of theology were founded wherein rabbis were trained and the sacred books interpreted.

Yet, in spite of all this, religion had declined. The inner spirit had disappeared. No religious prophet spoke for God, calling the nation to repentance. Christians today, who wish to be entertained more than to be energized by the living Christ, could well take note of the corresponding times in which Jesus lived.

The Pharisees, numbering some 6,000, believed in the separation of Jews from other peoples. They were the segregationists of their day. Zealous patriots willing to lay down their lives for the independence of their country, they hated the foreign yoke of Rome.

Because the Pharisees were of the middle class, the uneducated lower classes admired the philosophical pronouncements of the Pharisees.

The Scribes belonged to this group, too. They interpreted the Scriptures. They developed many peculiarities. Intent on multiplying laws until they included every detail of life — personal, domestic, and social — they even had a law which told people how to wash their hands.

The Sadducees were the wealthier people. They demanded a return to the Hebrew Scriptures and nothing but the Hebrew Scriptures and ridiculed the Pharisaical exclusiveness. They cried out for morality, yet they were skeptical, cold-hearted, worldly people. They mingled with Gentiles, enjoyed foreign products, and thought it was useless to fight for the freedom of their country.

Below all this, there was a large layer of people who had lost all contact with religion — the publicans (tax collectors), the harlots, and sinners.

It is into this world our Lord was born. He knew the times in which He lived. He was able to speak to it. As they referred to him, "Can anything good come out of Nazareth?" (John 1:46). Jesus knew the sin of his town and country and gave his life as a sacrifice for sin. In the Old Testament we read, "Father!" cried Isaac to his father, Abraham, "The fire and the wood are here, but where is the lamb for a burnt offering?" (Genesis 22:7). God provided the sacrifice. In the New Testament we hear John the Baptist crying out and pointing to Christ, "Here is the lamb of God who takes away the sin of the world" (John 1:29).

Among John the Baptist's hearers was Jesus. Jesus presented himself as a candidate for baptism. John drew back. He felt he was not worthy of even unlatching Jesus' sandal. But it was Jesus who had come to receive the "sacrament" of Baptism. He was baptized. And a voice from heaven said, "This is my Son, the Beloved, with whom I am well pleased" (Matthew 3:17).

Jesus used Scripture, a "means of grace." While only a boy, He spent three days in the Temple asking questions of learned people. Jesus' sayings, which are full of quotations from the Old Testament, give us insight to his study of the Hebrew Scriptures. When called upon in his hometown to read the Scriptures, He could unfold the rolls of papyri and quickly locate the Scripture to be read.

Jesus' preaching was couched in the sayings of old. His doctrine took the people from formalism to faith, from tradition to truth. He was able to repel the assaults of his opponents by quoting the prophets.

Jesus used Scripture at the time of his temptations. In that frightful struggle He said, "One does not live by bread alone, but by every word that comes from the mouth of God."

"Again it is written, 'Do not put the Lord your God to the test.' "

"Away with you, Satan! For it is written, 'Worship the Lord your God and serve only him.' " (See Matthew 4:1-11.)

It was then the devil left him. Scripture sustained Jesus. Does it not also sustain us?

Is your Lenten camera still rolling? Do you see that this preparation of Our Lord to proclaim the Word involved humility? Possessions can possess us. Our Lord did not live like the Romans. Although born in history, an incontestable fact, history is contained in him. A manual worker became our Messiah.

Do you see through the camera that this preparation of Jesus involved thoughtful study? He struggled to know truth. He understood history. He unveiled shallow religious practices. He pierced Pharasaism. He saw through the sham of the Sadducees. Can we recognize ourselves, too, in the times of Jesus as well as in our own time?

Do you see through your Lenten lens that this preparation of Jesus involved diligent use of the "means of grace"? He fought temptation with the Scriptures. He received the "sacrament" of baptism, and the voice of the Father declared his messiahship.

See through your Lenten lens true God and true man. Let the preparation of Jesus for down-to-earth living drive you to your knees in preparation to receive his body and blood. Let the faith, which He freely gives, flow through your Lenten camera so that your eyes behold "... the Lamb of God who takes away the sin of the world."

---

1. *Lutheran Book Of Worship*, Hymn 316, text: attr. Bernard of Clairvaux, 1091-1153.

Questions For Discussion

1) What kind of film is required for our Lenten camera?

2) What was the political situation in Jesus' time?

3) Define the roles of the following: Sanhedrin; Pharisees; Scribes; Sadducees.

4) What was the religious situation in Jesus' time?

5) Is daily scripture reading necessary? If so, why?

6) What is meant by "true God" and "true man"?

7) What can we do to keep our Lenten camera rolling?

2. Ministry Midst Obscurity

Scripture Reading: John 1:35-51

Prayer: Let us talk with God:
   O Father, give us hearts like the heart of Jesus Christ — hearts more ready to minister than to be ministered unto; hearts moved by compassion toward all people, especially toward little known people; hearts set upon the coming of Thy kingdom in the world of people; hearts eager to hear; hearts ready to love as Our Lord loved. Amen.

† † †

Since Johannes Gutenberg's printing of the first book in Europe from movable type in the fifteenth century and his masterpiece the *Mazarin Bible*, the general populace has been treated to a generous amount of information. By the middle of the nineteenth century, stereotype plates curved to form parts of cylinders were invented. Leading newspapers of yesterday used this basic principle in printing. Now lasers do the job. The modern press is a powerful instrument in molding the mind of the nation, as we can attest when we pick up the morning newspaper.

Shortly after the first World War, radio was developed and perfected. I remember listening to Lindbergh's safe landing in Paris by what was then called a "crystal set." In recent years television has brought into our living rooms and dens world events as they are occurring. When the television set goes awry, we can hardly wait until it is repaired or replaced, so much has it become a part of our lives.

Now in the computer age, we can contact people across the world via the Internet. E-mail delivers our messages instead of the door-to-door postman. We can bank, make deals, and pay our income taxes by computer.

Even the Church has not let communication go unnoticed. Bishops have E-mail numbers as well as Fax numbers. Magazines of churches publish stories on almost every subject, including sex, informing members about what is happening in the world of religion.

Too bad that Jesus did not have a computer or a cellular telephone and all the other gadgets during his first year in the ministry! The Synoptic Gospels (Matthew, Mark, and Luke — called synoptic because of their similarity) hardly mention his first year of ministry. Even John's gospel leaves eight months of that first year in the dark. Why? We can only surmise. Like any new personality on the scene, it took time for the public to take note of him. Yet, no one in history has done so much in three years as Jesus Christ.

His first year in the ministry causes us to rethink the meaning of the call into the ministry. Ministers, upon a call from a congregation, are ordained; that is, set apart to proclaim the Word and administer the Sacraments. Prior to ordination, they feel led by God to enter this high calling, sometimes experiencing the call in a dramatic way, as Samuel did; still others find it difficult to pinpoint a specific time. Even for Jesus, we cannot point to a definite time when He felt more of the pull of the ministry. He was born to be a preacher. He was inquisitive as a youth. He grew in wisdom and stature. His baptism was an affirmation of a life open to the influence of the Heavenly Father. When the Voice spoke, "This is my beloved Son," it was like the laying on of hands in our ordination service. His wilderness experience with terrifying temptations and successful interpetation and application of Scripture, which put Satan behind him, was seminary training at its best.

In a congregation I was serving, a young lady, led by the Holy Spirit to the conclusion that God wanted her to become a pastor, confessed there had been a gnawing in her heart for years, which she could no longer ignore. Some pastor's life of dedication influenced her. Wasn't there a John the Baptist in the life of our Lord?

Young people, flirting with the thought of entering the ministry, often wish for a bolt of lightning to strike, informing them of the will of God. As a consequence, a possible call is put on Will Call and never picked up. A bolt of lightning did strike Martin Luther in his call to the ministry. But it doesn't usually happen that way.

The call of the ministry can come from hearing the proclamation of the Word. The call can come through baptism, through victory over temptation, through a wilderness of conflicting vocational attractions which call for decision. Any young person contemplating the ministry, or any older person (for our seminaries report an increasing number of people who change vocations in their thirties, forties, and fifties), could well contemplate the life of our Lord. He did not ask for a voice from heaven; He became the voice of heaven. From Bethlehem to Calvary, his life was open to the touch of the Father. He set his face and feet toward the people of Palestine. Palestine was the scene of Jesus' earthly ministry.

A successful English preacher reminds the preacher that the world is his/her parish as Tom Allan wrote in *The Face Of My Parish*. Allan quoted from George Bernanos' book *The Diary Of A Country Priest*. The young priest, coming to his first parish, wrote these words in his notebook:

> *I know that my parish is a reality, that we belong to each other for all eternity: it is not a mere administration fiction, but a living cell in the everlasting Church. But if only the good God would open my eyes and unseal my ears ... these would be the eyes of all Christianity, of all parishes — perhaps of the poor human race itself. Our Lord saw them from the Cross....*[1]

But Jesus saw his parish from the ground first before He saw it from the cross. Palestine was his parish. What was it like?

Such a small parish, only a little larger than some of our states, covering an area of 10,434 square miles along the eastern end of the Mediterranean Sea, between Egypt and Syria. Only 150 miles long and less than 75 miles wide at its widest part at the southern end, it is insignificant as far as size is concerned.

However, it was strategically situated. Before Europe was developed, the great centers of civilization were in the Nile basin and in the Tigris-Euphrates Valley. Palestine lay on the only feasible overland route between the two centers. To the east was the uncrossable Arabian Desert. Trade, consequently, followed the Mediterranean coast. One of the caravan routes to the sea from the interior of Arabia crossed northern Palestine. Because of its location, Palestine was of enormous political significance.

It was Sir George Adam Smith, Scottish biblical scholar and Hebraist, who coined the expression, "Palestine was the bridge of Asia."[2] The parish of Our Lord was not in a remote corner. It was the center of the ancient world. Nations of the world vied for her control, even as they still do today.

In climate and rainfall, Palestine is semi-tropical, corresponding to the southern end of California and northern Lower California. In the winter the temperature rarely falls below freezing, and in the summer the hottest days frequently have a temperature of over 100 degrees.

In Jesus' time, industry in the Dead Sea region produced a form of salt. Agriculture was the most stable occupation but because of the uncertainty of sufficient rainfall it was unpredictable. Fruit-growing orchards covered the valleys and terraced hillsides. From the sheep and goats the people got their milk and cheese and wool.

Our Lord knew his parish. His parables sparkle with everyday scenes. His preaching was relevant. He knew the sight of the caravan. He recalled the political foes who had pillaged and divided the land and peoples. He ate of the fruit of the vine and drank the milk of the goat. His back bore the cloth made of wool. His compassion for his people in Palestine was genuine. He was one of them. This true God became a person on earth.

After Jesus' baptism and wilderness experience, Jesus once more came to the bank of the Jordan where John was preaching. How great this man, John! What humility! He knew who he was and what his role was. John said, "He (Jesus) must increase, but I must decrease" (John 3:30). Furthermore, some of John's followers immediately became followers of Jesus.

One of the first things Jesus did was to select his church board — the disciples. What is a disciple? A disciple is a learner and follower and assists in spreading the Good News. The twelve disciples comprised the inner circle of Christ's followers, people he could depend on to further the understanding of the kingdom of God.

What kind of disciples did Jesus choose? The religious leaders were in Jerusalem: there He would find the scribes and theologians capable of interpreting the Scriptures. A young preacher could use an experienced, intelligent sage of the Scriptures.

In Jerusalem, Jesus would find the Sadducees, the wealthier religious people. He might need one of them. A wealthy person could do him some good. A young preacher could use money to carry on his program.

In Jerusalem, Jesus could find a political figure that might help his cause. Think of it! If He could latch onto a Roman prelate, convert him, his cause could spread immediately to the Gentile world, perhaps even to Rome. His parish could be multiplied!

Where did Jesus go to enlist his church board? He went down by the seashore and selected people. "Follow me, and I will make you fish for people," He said. And Matthew reports, "Immediately they left their nets and followed Him" (Matthew 4:19, 20). "Andrew, Simon Peter, John, Philip, Nathanael — Come, follow me!" And they did. There was a magnetism about the Master.

Jesus did not go into the big city of Jerusalem to find disciples. He looked for people of a very common, ordinary life, who could do the extraordinary — follow when others were content with the status quo in religion; people who knew something about the coming of the Messiah; people not caged by tradition; people unafraid to launch out into a new work, and not fearful of the word "change."

The Gospels give me the impression that all Jesus did in selecting disciples was to walk around and point a finger at somebody, as if He chose the disciples right and left without too much thought. On further consideration, however, I have a strong hunch that Jesus stalked every one of them and knew them well before He issued a call, as He commented about the attributes of Nathanael. " 'Here is truly an Israelite in whom there is no deceit!' Nathanael asked him, 'Where did you get to know me?' Jesus answered, 'I saw you under the fig tree before Phililp called you' " (John 1:47, 48).

In brief, Jesus called people of faith! As John reports, "We have found him about whom Moses in the law and also the prophets wrote, Jesus son of Joseph out of Nazareth" (John 1:45). Nathanael had questions: " 'Can anything good come out of Nazareth?' Philip said to him, 'Come and see' " (John 1:46). Nathanael was found by the Messiah and followed him, as did all twelve when called. No one hesitated. Jesus knew whom to choose.

The modern church can learn a lesson or two from Jesus. Select women and men of faith and spiritual insight to serve as leaders in the congregation. A person of intelligence is not enough. A person of wealth is not enough. A person of power and political influence and popularity is not enough. Of course, select women and men of intelligence and wealth and influence, but be sure first of all that they are women and men of faith and spiritual insight, ardent believers in the head of the Church, Jesus Christ. But also go after the common, ordinary people of this world and teach them to "fish for people." Anybody here listening to the Call of Christ to follow "... in his train"?[3]

William Lazareth, in the Hein-Fry Lectures of 1995, painted a picture of the Church that is frightening: that the Church is not lifting up Christ and is giving people only what they want. He reviewed Luther's Large Catechism and made a call for the Church to come back to Christ.

I wonder how Jesus felt after his first year? Only three incidents in that year are worth recording, and some scholars are not so sure they occurred in the first year. Most, however, agree there were these three:

1) At Cana in Galilee Jesus attended a wedding. He didn't even perform the ceremony. But He did change water into wine, the first of his miracles. A few followed him after that. It should be remembered that Jesus never performed a miracle in order to entertain or impress his congregation. His purpose was always to glorify his Father.

A man was asked, "Do you believe Jesus Christ actually changed water into wine?" "I don't know," he replied, "but I do know that He changed alcohol into furniture, concern for self into concern for family, hate into love. This I do know: Jesus Christ changed me!"

2) At the Temple in Jerusalem, Jesus drove out the money changers. The city was crowded with people who had come to celebrate the Passover. How could they worship God and money at the same time? The Temple had become not a house of prayer but a house of profiteering.

Today, the Church still debates the merit of commercialism. From bingo to fund-raisers, good causes in the name of Christ trick well-meaning people into thinking they are doing something for God while they are only going through the motions of religion, akin to Jesus' time. Any church which cannot live on the faith and love gifts of its members is not worth saving.

3) The nighttime interview with Nicodemus. It must have seemed a hopeful sign for Jesus when a Pharisee, one of the heads of the religious nation, came in a spirit of humility to Jesus and said to him, "Rabbi, we know that you are a teacher who has come from God; for no one can do these signs that you do apart from the presence of God." Jesus' reply was plain and to the point: "You must be born from above." (See John 3:1-21.) No other Pharisee came to be born anew; only Nicodemus. Anybody here ready to hear the Call of Christ to renew commitment to the Lord of all? That is what Lent is all about.

James Stalker in his book on *The Life Of Christ* calls this first year "The Year Of Obscurity." He is right. A few followers, a miracle, a burst of excitement at the Temple, and one Pharisee moved to deeper insight. The world of Christ did not feel the impact of his first year in the ministry. But, Jesus knew what He was doing. He was about his Father's business, as true God and true man.

1. Tom Allan, *The Face Of My Parish*, p. 9.

2. *Historical Geography Of The Holy Land* (New York: Harper and Row, 1966), p. 6.

3. *Lutheran Book of Worship*, Hymn 183, text: Reginald Heber, 1783-1826, alt.

Questions For Discussion

1) What is a "call"? Are only clergy called?

2) What is ordination?

3) Why was Palestine considered politically significant?

4) What is a parish? Where was Jesus' parish?

5) What is a disciple? An apostle? What is the difference?

6) What type of follower did Jesus select? What qualifications are necessary to be a church leader today?

7) Name three incidents in Jesus' first year of ministry.

3. Ministry Midst Popularity

Scripture Reading: Mark 5

Prayer: Let us talk with God:
Dear Lord, For these three things we pray; To see Thee more clearly, To love Thee more dearly, To follow Thee more nearly, day by day. (Saint Richard)

† † †

After seeing the famous statue of Venus de Milo, which was armless when found on the Island of Melos in 1820, likely the work of a Hellenistic sculptor of the second or third century before Christ, and left unrestored by its French owners, I could better understand the experience of Heinrich Heine. Heine was a brilliant writer who suffered from paralysis of the spinal cord. He wanted to take one last look at the goddess of beauty. With great effort Heine dragged himself to the Louvre in Paris and lay a long while at the feet of the lady of Milo (Melos). He said, "... The goddess did look down compassionately on me, but with so little comfort that it seemed as if she would say, 'Dost thou not see that I have no arms, and therefore cannot help thee?' "

Does not that experience of Heine with the goddess of beauty, Venus de Milo, stir our memory to recall how in contrast little children were brought to our Lord "... in order that he might lay his hands on them and pray" (Matthew 19:13)? No little child, no anguished person ever felt about our Lord like Heine felt about Venus de Milo.

In our hour of greatest need, things which have been a great help to us throughout life — art, science, literature, music — are unable to support us. They have no arms. Only the arms of Jesus can sustain us. "Come to me, all you that are weary and are carrying heavy burdens, and I will give you rest" (Matthew 11:28).

The people of the province of Galilee, the northern part of Palestine, came to know this compassionate Jesus. He was able to take up into his arms the diseased and the discouraged and heal them. His ministry among them covers his second year in the ministry.

Galilee was sixty miles long and thirty miles wide, covering no more of a territory than an ordinary county. For the most part it was an elevated plateau although irregular mountains varied the scene. Near the eastern boundary there was a sudden dip into a great gulf through which flowed the Jordan River. Then at 500 feet below the Mediterranean, in the middle of this great gulf, there was the harp-shaped Sea of Galilee. While on this sea, I had to get on the deck of the boat. I wanted to feel the breeze of the Sea as Jesus and his disciples must have felt it while fishing.

The province was very fertile. Large villages and towns were spotted everywhere. But the center of activity was the basin of the lake, thirteen miles long and six miles wide. On the western shore, the mountains sloped enough for cultivation. By the eastern shore, a quarter of a mile back, high bare hills stood out. At the northern end of the lake was the Plain of Gennesareth, which was broadened by the delta of the river and where many streams from the hills made it a land of fertility and beauty. One author suggests that it is so fertile that if not tended it would turn into a jungle of thorn and oleander.

This plain contained the chief cities on the lake, such as Capernaum, Bethsaida, and Chorazin. Thousands of people lived there. Since the highways from Egypt to Damascus and from Phoenicia to the Euphrates passed through, this territory was a great center of traffic. Hundreds of fishing boats moved across the lake. The whole region reflected energy and prosperity.

Capernaum became the new home of Jesus. From it He could journey inland to the west or He could visit the villages by the lake. Sometimes He would take a boat to the eastern shore and visit there. He would go back to Capernaum for a day or two or perhaps a week or two at a time.

Because the whole province was so accessible, within weeks Jesus' name was on the lips of the people. He became the subject of conversation on the fishing boats and in the streets of the villages and towns. Crowds began to gather about him. They multiplied into the thousands. They followed him wherever He went. The news spread beyond Galilee to Judea and Peraea, even to Idumaea in the far south, and to Tyre and Sidon in the far north. The crowds became so large that He had to take them out of the narrow streets of the towns to the fields and deserts. He spoke from the shore of the sea. Galilee became on fire with excitement. Why? Because of his miracles and his preaching.

If you had lived in Galilee, you would have heard about the Gadarenes. These were men so savage that nobody could go along the road near them. One of them had been bound with chains on his hands and feet, but he tore them apart. No one was strong enough to control him.

This same man saw Jesus at a distance and ran out to him, screeching and threatening. Jesus said, "Come out of the man, you unclean spirit!" (Mark 5:1-20). The whole town went out to see what happened. Two thousand hogs had plunged into the lake and were drowned. The evil spirit had gone out of the man into the hogs. They found the man, previously besieged by mental problems, now sitting at the feet of Jesus, cleanly dressed and in his right mind.

If you had lived in Galilee, you would have seen or heard of the daughter of Jairus. Jairus was a leader in the synagogue. He pleaded with Jesus to come and heal his daughter. She was only twelve years of age and was dying. On the way to the little girl, a woman touched the tassel of Jesus' gament and was healed. Meantime the little girl died. Already the flute players and the paid mourners had gathered. Jesus said the little girl was not dead but asleep. They ridiculed him. Jesus took the child's hand and called, " 'Talitha, cum' which means 'Little girl, get up' " (Mark 5:41). And she did.

If you had lived in Galilee, you would have seen or heard about two blind men receiving their sight and about a man who could not speak but now could talk. You would have heard about Jesus walking on water, stilling a storm, and feeding thousands.

Who is this Jesus of Nazareth? Nazareth did not claim him. When He stood up in the synagogue to read scripture and claimed to be the fulfillment of prophecy, they picked up stones to throw at him. But the rest of Galilee claimed him. He gathered the people in his arms and healed them. He stretched his arms across the sea and it calmed. This God-man had arms that stretched out to enfold humankind.

Not only his miracles, which called for faith and revealed his divinity, but his preaching drew the people.

Jesus knew the power of speech. The barbarians had their storytellers. The Greeks and Romans listened to their orators. And the Jews prized speech almost above everything. They revered their prophets.

What was Jesus' preaching like? He was a Jew. The oriental mind likes to linger on a single point, turning it round and round, making a few concise, crisp statements, and then going on to another point which may not have direct connection. The western mind likes to create a chain of thought with an introduction, three points, and a conclusion.

Jesus' preaching and teaching was that of the oriental mind. Yet He did not speak like the rabbis, who droned on and on about how far you could walk on the sabbath or the nature of certain laws. Many a congregation must have gone to sleep while the rabbis talked, as some people do in our churches today! When I was a child, ushers used to have a long pole and poked people when they went to sleep. Now they ought to poke the preacher!

In contrast, Jesus did not speak on the usual doctrines. He came to "fulfil the law." He never wrote a book. He came "proclaiming the good news of God, and saying 'The time is fulfilled, and the kingdom of God has come near; repent, and believe in the good news' " (Mark 1:14, 15). It was Paul who said God is pleased "through the foolishness of our proclamation, to save those who believe" (1 Corinthians 1:21).

The people said, "Never has anyone spoken like this!" (John 7:46). He spoke in figures of speech. His preaching was alive with the aspects of the country and the life of the times. He spoke of the lilies of the field, the sheep following the shepherd, the narrow gate of the city, the virgins with their lamps waiting in the darkness for the wedding procession, the Pharisee and the publican in church, the rich man seated in his palace at a feast, and the beggar lying at his gate with the dogs licking his sores.

But the main characteristic of Jesus' preaching was the parable. He took an incident from common life and pictured it with a corresponding higher, nobler truth. These parables stuck in the memory as illustrations do from the modern preacher's sermon. Who can forget the parables of the prodigal, the sower, the Good Samaritan? Can you remember as well passages in Homer, in Virgil, in Dante, or in Shakespeare? Jesus' speech was simple yet profound. "The crowds were astounded at his teaching, for he taught them as one having authority, and not as their scribes" (Matthew 7:28, 29).

The Bible mentions other qualities: boldness – "Lo, he speaks boldly" (John 7:26 KJV); power — "For his word was with power" (Luke 4:32 KJV); graciousness — "All spoke well of him and were amazed at the gracious words that came from his mouth" (Luke 4:22).

Jesus spoke often of "the kingdom of God." People wondered where to look for it. Jesus said that the kingdom is within you. He raised the kingdom above time and circumstance. He invited all races and classes, the rich and the poor, the Jew and the Gentile, to receive God's power in human life.

Not only did the arms of Christ reach out to enfold people but also his voice: "... as for what was sown on good soil, this is the one who hears the word and understands it, who indeed bears fruit and yields, in one case a hundredfold, in another sixty, and in another thirty" (Matthew 13:23).

The chief danger then, and today, is that of accepting Christ's words without accepting him. "There is all the difference in the world," said Eric Frost, "between Zeus coming down *disguised* as a man and God *becoming* man in Jesus. God perceived that to redeem mankind he had not merely to come amongst us; he had to get *into* our race."[1]

So Jesus spoke to multitudes and individuals, on a mountain, by the seashore, along the highway, in the synagogue, in the Temple courts. He instructed a small group of followers called disciples. He divided his hearers such as in the parables of the sower, the tares and the wheat, and the wedding feast. His work was so extensive that he hardly had time to eat and sleep.

In this second year Jesus was notoriously popular. Thousands upon thousands came to hear him or to see a miracle. Even at that some Galileans were repelled. Others heard with wonder in their hearts without conviction of the heart. Still others heard and were affected for a time but soon returned to their old interests and old ways.

The statue of Venus de Milo is beautiful. But it has no arms and no voice. People are known today to worship things or even art or science or literature or music. Anything which demands and gets our only interest and devotion is our god.

What would you do if Jesus Christ came into your Galilee? Into your bailiwick? Would He just be your favorite healer or most popular preacher? Your favorite storyteller?

Charles Lamb, English essayist (1775-1834), and his friends were discussing what they would do and say if certain poets or kings should walk into their room. Finally someone asked, "What would you do if Jesus Christ should walk in?" There was a pause. It was Lamb who said, "If Shakespeare should walk in we would all stand; if Jesus Christ should walk in we would all kneel."

A statue only represents life. A poet and king are only figures in history. Jesus is true God as we confess in the Nicene Creed. Christ is the way, the truth, and the life! He is the savior of the world. "At the name of Jesus every knee should bend, in heaven and on earth and under the earth, and every tongue should confess that Jesus Christ is Lord, to the glory of God the Father" (Philippians 2:10, 11).

---

1. Eric Frost, *This Jesus* (Great Neck, Long Island, NY: Channel Press, 1959). p. 49.

Questions For Discussion

1) What sustains us in our greatest hours of need?

2) Describe Galilee.

3) What is a miracle? Name some of Jesus' miracles and cite the significance of each.

4) Who were the Gadarenes?

5) What is preaching? What was unique about Jesus' preaching? What good is preaching?

6) What is a parable? Name some of Jesus' parables and cite the significance of each.

7) What is meant by "kingdom of God"?

8) Who is Jesus?

4. Ministry Midst Opposition

Scripture Reading: Matthew 23

Prayer: Let us talk with God:
Search us deeply, O God, that in remembering Jesus Christ Our Lord, our minds and hearts may be cleansed of all insecurities, of self-righteous poses, and of dubious devotions. Show us the great glory of him who lived so faithfully and died so humbly in revealing your love.

Grant us no peace in idle meditations but thrust us, by the Holy Spirit, into the very life of our time and town, that with seeing eyes and open minds we may love, as you have so loved us through the cross of Jesus Christ. Amen.

† † †

It is hard for a Christian to imagine anyone so displeased with the disposition and dedication of Jesus Christ as to oppose him.

We can understand why Nero was opposed, why Napoleon was exiled, why Luther was brought to Worms. But, who could find a flaw in the life and teaching of Christ? We can understand why John Wilkes Booth, the assassin of Lincoln, could be in disrepute; why Hitler could be cursed; and why Saddam Hussein could be opposed in a Gulf War; but, who could be so displeased with Jesus to oppose him? There were some who did.

What caused the change in Christ's popularity? One cause was the role of the Sadducees and Herodians. These politically-minded people paid little attention to Jesus in the beginning of his ministry. They were too engrossed in their own affairs: money, court courtesies and procedures, social life, and amusements.

How the general public reacted to a prophet mattered little to them. If He could entertain them and maintain their interest, so much the better. It would give the people something to occupy their thoughts. It would permit the Sadducees and Herodians time to carry on their civic and social affairs, since they represented the vested interests of Jews in Jerusalem.

Although they disagreed with the beliefs of the Pharisees, when the Pharisees and scribes began to paint a picture of a possible political revolt as a result of Jesus' preaching and healing, the Sadducees and Herodians (supporters of Herod Antipas) took a closer look into the matter. They did not want another John the Baptist on their hands. They didn't want any occurrence which would light a fuse for a revolution. Their interest and curiosity put a political slant on the situation. As a consequence, the common people became more and more fearful of following such a prophet.

We have Sadducees today. They are people far more interested in the stock market than in the Savior of humankind; far more concerned about the national debt than in human values; far more interested in sports than in making disciples; far more enthralled with clubs, eating out, and television than by the Church of Jesus Christ.

We have Herodians today. They are the politically-minded people whose chief concern is getting their man in the White House, rather than who will accept Jesus Christ as Savior-God; more concerned with power struggles than with the power of the Holy Spirit.

Give Sadducees and Herodians enough newspaper space and television time and they will not care what happens to individuals. But, if the Church should speak out on social issues, watch them talk about the separation of church and state. "Stick to the Bible, Padre, and stay out of politics!"

Thus, Jesus was looked upon as revolutionary, which He was in a sense. They didn't understand He was their Redeemer. The Sadducees and Herodians didn't want him to change their lifestyles. They spoke out against Christ. He was a threat. They opposed him.

The Pharisees and scribes naturally took deep interest in what was happening. They were in charge of ecclesiastical affairs. They were the clergy and leading lay people of their day. It was their responsibility to nurture the people in laws and doctrines. They were the Bible readers and interpreters of Scripture. They were the custodians of religious truth. Why would they oppose Jesus? Of all people, they should have supported him!

From the very first, the Pharisees looked upon Jesus with suspicion. They were puzzled by this traveling evangelist who went up and down their land and stirred hearts hungry for fresh understanding of God. They sent deputations to check on Jesus' ministry, weighing every situation. They discussed his sermons and teachings, analyzed each word, every expression. In their theological classrooms the doctrines of Jesus were debated, his miracles analyzed and dissected. They came to the conclusion that they must oppose him. Their judgment became warped by clinging to tradition. They were not open to change. Why?

Jesus was so unlike their concept of a messiah. Surely the Messiah would grow up in Judea, get his education in Jerusalem, and be like one of them. It was impossible for them to accept a messiah born in a stable, reared in a little village of Galilee, and without a formal education.

Furthermore, they had no respect for his disciples. They were not from their kind. Why, these fellows were nothing but common laborers! All they knew about was mending nets and catching fish. They were daydreamers. And when Jesus selected Matthew, a tax collector, to be one of his followers — that did it! Anyone knows that a tax collector cannot get into the kingdom. A tax collector is an insult to society, a leech on the economy of every decent citizen.

In addition to these things which prejudiced their minds, Jesus didn't follow their rituals to the letter. He permitted his disciples to gather grain while walking through a field on the sabbath. He even healed on the sabbath! His disciples didn't wash their hands according to Jewish law. In fact, Jesus did not conform to their teachings. He lost his temper in the Temple. He became infuriated with the lifestyle of Pharisees and called them hypocrites. Jesus was accused of being slanderous.

By this time the Pharisees and scribes were so set againt him, their ears were not open to understand his messianic claims nor their eyes open to believe his power. They turned off their hearing aids! They closed their eyes. They tuned him out. Besides, miracles were no proof of divinity. Many a prophet had demonstrated unusual powers. And when Jesus associated with publicans, harlots, and sinners, they chalked up Jesus as a false prophet, perhaps a lunatic prophet.

The same thing can happen to any Church which becomes ingrown. Calloused by worldliness, uninspired by shallow spirituality, the Pharisees' and scribes' hearts were deadened to a new voice and a new vision. So they poisoned the public against Jesus. They planted suspicion in the minds of the Sadducees and Herodians that Jesus was a deceiver and a dangerous person.

Even the contemporary Church can oppose Christ. From countless pulpits we hear what is pleasing to the people instead of the power unto salvation. One minister's sermon was titled "The Upside-Down Wheelbarrow." One minister quizzed another about what he thought about that and his reply was, "There mustn't be much in it!"

Many a congregation today does not want to hear about sin or the need of repentance or the gospel implications of nuclear power, abortion, divorce, refugees, world hunger, the questions of the day, hiding behind a personal religion which in essence is afraid to take on life. From numerous congregations lay people are heard to excuse themselves from introducing Christ to another person because they claim they do not know enough about their religion. Pray tell, when did ignorance become a good reason for not learning? What in the world are we doing in the Church of today if we are not equipping people to pass on the Good News?

I liked what I saw on a chiropractor's office door as I went out: "If you feel better than when you came in, tell somebody." Isn't that what the business of the Church is — to tell somebody about the joy of being a follower of Jesus Christ, true God?

In the Church today we need to be alert to all the dangers of shoving Jesus Christ out the door. No tradition is good enough unless it sets people on fire. No trumped-up reason for watering down the gospel is sufficient reason to merit opposition to truth. If a church or an individual is challenged to leap daringly forward, a challenge within capability, people should rejoice. Several years ago in a ministerial meeting I heard a pastor say, "The greatest opposition a pastor has is not from the world but from his own people." How sad!

The Pharisees and scribes were Jesus' own people. Yet, they opposed him. He was too radical. They grew to hate him enough to want to do away with him.

But what about the people in Galilee who responded to him and came out by the thousands? They had come to compare Jesus to the greatest of their prophets. They asked, "Is He Isaiah or Jeremiah or even Elijah risen from the dead?"

One incident turned them against him. Sometimes that's all it takes. People harbor misconceptions.

Jesus took a boat to the northeastern tip of the Sea of Galilee. There on the grassy plains of Bethsaida He fed thousands of people with a few fish and a little bread. The crowd became electrified! They decided to make him King and wanted to put a crown on his head. At last, they felt, the long awaited leader had come and they were ready for revolt!

In that moment, Jesus could have done anything with that crowd. All of Galilee would have turned toward him. But in that moment Jesus saw the shallow results of his ministry among them. At first they thought of him as a great prophet; now, a political deliverer. That's all. What a blow!

He refused to accept their offered crown. Scripture records, "Because of this many of his disciples turned back and no longer went about with him" (John 6:66).

How this must have crushed the heart of Jesus. He was truly the "Man of Sorrows." The lame walked; the blind were given eyes to see; minds were cured; broken hearts were healed. But when Jesus did not fulfil their wish, He was rejected.

"So Jesus asked the twelve, 'Do you also wish to go away?' Simon Peter answered him, 'Lord, to whom can we go? You have the words of eternal life. We have come to believe and know that you are the Holy One of God' " (John 6:67-69).

Have you rejected Jesus, the true God, somewhere along the way? Is your faith in him as strong today as when you first believed? Has anything gotten in the way?

And do you feel rejected? How do you react when opposed?

Jesus Christ was rejected and opposed by the wealthy, by the politicians, by the religious people of the day, and by the crowds. What was left? A handful of disciples and a few hundred adherents.

What did Jesus do? He went up to a mountain and prayed. He came down from that mountain and instructed his faithful followers, prepared them for further rejection and opposition. He never faltered from the purpose for which He was sent — to redeem the people of the world.

When you are rejected and opposed be sure the purpose for which you stand is worthy. Then, in the heat of battle, go up to a mountain or go into a closet and pray. God has never yet deserted one of his followers.

God did not desert Moses at the Red Sea: "Do not be afraid, stand firm, and see the deliverance that the Lord will accomplish for you today ..." (Exodus 14:13).

God did not desert the disciples: "But during the night an angel of the Lord opened the prison doors, brought them out, and said, 'Go, stand in the Temple and tell the people the whole message about this life' " (Acts 5:19-20).

God did not desert Paul and Silas: "About midnight Paul and Silas were praying and singing hymns to God, and the prisoners were listening to them. Suddenly there was an earthquake, so violent that the foundations of the prison were shaken; and immediately all the doors were opened and everyone's chains were unfastened" (Acts 16:25-26).

God did not desert Martin Luther when he said: "My conscience is captive to the Word of God ... Here I stand, I cannot do otherwise."[1]

It was the fearless, opposed Christ who encouraged his disciples as He departed from them, "Remember, I am with you always, to the end of the age" (Matthew 28:20).

Then, why should you or I ever fear rejection or opposition? Our true God will sustain us!

---

1. Roland H. Bainton, *Here I Stand, A Life of Martin Luther* (Nashville: Abingdon, 1950), p. 185.

Questions For Discussion

1) Why was Jesus opposed and who opposed him?

2) How did people in Jesus' day perceive the coming of the Messiah? How do we?

3) What comparisons could be drawn between the church of Jesus' day and the church of today?

4) How do you react when opposed?

5) How can conflict be handled in a congregation?

6) Who is the authority in a congregation?

5. Ministry Midst Decision

Scripture Reading: John 12:20-33

Prayer: Let us talk with God:
"Now the day is over; Night is drawing nigh;
Shadows of the evening Steal across the sky,
Jesus, give the weary Calm and sweet repose
With your tend'rest blessing May our eyelids close."[1]
   Amen.

† † †

I don't know if you heard this special newscast or not. Walter Cronkite, a world traveler and famous newscaster who retired some years ago but still does special assignments, announced yesterday that Jesus of Nazareth, who lived almost 2,000 years ago, actually led a revolt against the Roman government, then in control of his native land of Palestine. Scrolls were found to support the fact, Cronkite stated, in a special CBS announcement.

The scrolls revealed that when 5,000 people were fed on the northeastern shore of the Sea of Galilee with a few fish and bread, a supposedly miraculous revelation of Jesus' divine power, one of the men in that vast crowd hurriedly made a makeshift crown and placed it upon his head. This began a demonstration that was not to end until it reached Jerusalem. It was the crowning achievement of Jesus' cleverly laid out political plan, cunningly engineered by a committee of twelve followers, headed by a big fisherman known as Peter.

The scrolls were discovered on a mountainside in the vicinity of where the so-called miracle of the feeding of the thousands took place. It is believed the scrolls were lodged there to commemorate the event. The scrolls further revealed that the campaign committee had organized several hundred people prior to the "miracle" to take along enough food for each one to serve ten people. When Jesus took the few loaves of bread and fish from a boy, selected and stationed to be next to Jesus when the "miracle" was to take place, a tribute to the genius of the committee and the idea of one called Andrew, the several hundred plotters in the plan took from their person the food which they had hidden inside their clothing and distributed it around so cleverly that it was thought all the food came by the hand of Jesus.

The scrolls record that Jesus accepted the crown offered by the cheering 5,000 and began a march on Jerusalem, gathering thousands of followers along the way, from Galilee through Samaria. Arriving in Judea, they were met by Roman soldiers who easily crushed the revolt. One of Jesus' right hand men, Peter, was effective with his sword, cutting off the ear of a soldier, but he and the poorly equipped, disorganized multitude were no match for the highly trained Roman soldiers. Jesus was then taken outside the gate of Jerusalem and executed, according to custom by crucifixion, along with two other political agitators not identified in the scrolls.

You can relax now. No such scrolls were found! Walter Cronkite did not make such an announcement. I wrote that story to sharpen our minds and quicken our hearts for a deeper look into the real character and nature of the Savior who lived among us.

Jesus did not come to set one political power against another. He came to reveal who God is. He came to die so that we might live.

How did He prepare to die? It isn't easy to face death. When a member of the congregation was going through that valley, we talked openly about death. She wanted to live but her body said "no." Frequently when we are around people who are about to die, we make small talk and joke a lot, never getting down to the dust from which we came. Shame on us when we are unwilling to talk about death as freely as we talk about life. Important decisons need to be made. Questions are to be answered. And I am not talking about funeral arrangements. I am talking about arrangements with God.

Arrangements for Jesus' death were made in eternity. He was literally born to die! Such a young man, full of life yet full of death. How did He prepare to die?

In his earthly life, Jesus was a person of decision. There was no wavering, no waffling, no piling up of excuses, no alibis day after day. His life was marked by decision after decision — preparing him for death. He had lived on sound principles ground out in the experience of the wilderness and his battle with Satan. Scripture was a part of the fabric of his life. He was determined to spend his life and not save it. He had high purpose. He did not compromise. He had made the decision to fulfill the promise of salvation. There was no backing up. There was no thought of self first. He emptied himself. He humbled himself. He gave himself. Nobody took his life. He gave it. His words ring out to us, "Those who find their life will lose it, and those who lose their life for my sake will find it" (Matthew 10:39). Jesus lost.

We live in an age wherein to be a winner is everything. We brag about having it all together. There is a time to be a loser. There is a time to let it all fall to pieces. People say, "I can't follow Christ and make a profit in my business." Some say, "I can't talk about my faith and keep my friends." When we start making such statements, we better take a second look at our stance in life. There is a time to stand alone. There is a time to stand on principle. There is a time to pay the price. Of belief!

And, there is a time for split-second decision. The time comes for all to make the decision of whether to accept the crown or to accept the consequences of standing on principle. There comes the time for on-the-spot decision. What has been going on in a life shows up at such a time in life. How a person reacts to crisis reveals what principles the person has been living on.

Jesus' life prepared him for making a decison which determined his destiny. When the crowd offered him a crown, it was not a difficult decision for him to turn it down. It would have been a boost to his ego and a boon to his popularity to wear the crown. But He didn't think in such terms. For the crowd to react to his teaching by offering him a crown was a ridiculous affront. In essence, it was an alarming situation which called for quick decision. His messianic consciousness did not permit him to accept a worldly crown. He turned it down.

No one in the crowd agreed with Jesus' decision. Five thousand voices claimed He was wrong. Even his disciples did not understand, especially Judas. He walked alone. A few who still believed He would choose another time and place to be king continued to follow. The decision of Christ, however, was based upon the ages: "It will be said on that day, Lo, this is our God; we have waited for him, so that he might save us. This is the Lord for whom we have waited; let us be glad and rejoice in his salvation" (Isaiah 25:9). This was not the day or the hour or the way. A kingly crown corrodes. Jesus was waiting for a more symbolic crown – thorns thrust into his head, a crown fit for a savior. He was a man of decision. The word *decision* itself means to settle, to choose. Jesus chose to go to Jerusalem and die.

Decisions are made by us each day in the week. Christian principles undergird us. Coming to grips with situations which call for decision tests our day-to-day storage of spiritual things and draws from us that which is in the reservoir of the soul. What is housed in our hearts and souls determines the nature of our decisions.

It was Jesus' decision to take his disciples away from crowds and school them in the way of salvation. In his last six months in Galilee, He abandoned to a degree his work of preaching and healing. He and the disciples traveled to Tyre and Sidon in the northwest along the Mediterranean Sea, to Caesarea-Philippi on the far northeast coast and to the Decapolis, south and east of the lake. Jesus asked his disciples questions about who He was and what they believed. His heart leaped with joy when Peter answered for all the disciples, "You are the Messiah" (Mark 8:29).

Jesus endeavored to prepare the disciples for his sufferings and death, the decision made in full awareness of his role as the Redeemer. The disciples could not fully fathom the depth of his teachings as He carefully detailed what would happen to him. They could not completely imagine the necessity of such a tragic event as the crucifixion. James and John argued about who would sit on the right and left of Jesus in his kingdom. They were still thinking of a crown. This God-man of decision, however, knew that later his teaching would serve them well. Reaching back into the Scriptures, Jesus stored in their hearts truths which would be of a soul-shaking nature, especially at the time of Pentecost.

In addition to being able to make a clear decision, Jesus prepared for his death by meeting conflict with courage. This was a pattern in his life. At least three times He clashed head-on with the Pharisees. The third clash involved the Pharisees' demand to show them a sign, something that would prove He had a right to teach the way He did. They wanted something similar to Moses' staff turning into a snake (Exodus 4) or his hand turned to leprosy and made whole again.

Jesus replied to the Pharisees: "An evil and adulterous generation asks for a sign, but no sign will be given to it except the sign of the prophet Jonah. For just as Jonah was three days and three nights in the belly of the sea monster, so for three days and three nights the Son of Man will be in the heart of the earth" (Matthew 12:39-40).

Jesus warned the disciples about hypocrisy in religion, about false teaching, and about false prophets. Can you not feel the sting of his words spoken to the Pharisees, "Therefore I tell you, the kingdom of God will be taken away from you and given to a people that produces the fruits of the kingdom" (Matthew 21:43)? Jesus met conflict with courage. Does it not take courage to do what is right today?

We demand signs today. We desire unmistakable proof. We demand of God some snake-charming event which will assure us of belief. Everyday situations crawl with a deeper cancer than cancer itself — hypocrisy and false assumptions. And, many a Christian has walked away from an opportunity to witness because he or she didn't have the heart to confront. It is easier to avoid a non-believer than to witness to a person. It takes courage to meet people head-on.

Jesus never saw with human eyes the fruit of his witness to Pharisees. There is no doubt their religion was shaken to its roots.

Palestine would never be the same, nor the world, because Christ met conflict with courage and clarity of thought. "No one was able to give him an answer, nor from that day did anyone dare to ask him any more questions" (Matthew 22:46).

Decisions can be made on our own. Even conflicts can be resolved by innate character or compromise. But a Christian prays about decisions to be made and conflicts to be solved. Prayer gives patience under fire and places divine wisdom over human reasoning.

In this period following the Galilean crisis, Christ spent much time in prayer. This was his lifelong practice and his source of strength. He could not face death without prayer. Now He was frequently alone. Yet in his busiest times, He still escaped from the crowds to talk with his Father. He prayed until He wept, so great was his anguish of heart. In the garden He asked his disciples, "So, could you not stay awake with me one hour?" (Matthew 26:40). Some of us have difficulty making room for that one hour a week when we are supposed to gather to pray.

His prayers were answered with the transfiguration. Who can understand it? But this experience of being in the company of the saints fortified him to go back into the valley where there was certain death.

Jesus left Galilee and spent six months on his way to Jerusalem. On his way He preached all over the land. Seventy disciples were sent ahead to prepare the villages and towns to hear him. The same enthusiastic reaction met him as at first in Galilee. He went to the far corners of Perea, to Samaria, on to the far banks of the Jordan, to the villages of Bethany and Ephraim.

During all his travels, prayer was his mainstay. This word *prayer* describes the life of Christ. The in-battle of the heart and mind were molded to meet Calvary. Calvary was his answer to prayer.

O, if our prayers could envelop the same concern for people as our Lord! O, if the answers to our prayers were as clearly understood and as dynamically acted upon! Mountains of indifference would disappear. Rivers of faith would flow freely. Hearts would be melted. Souls would be saved. If you want to know the power of prayer, pray as Christ did.

Walter Cronkite could have been instructed by a broadcasting station to describe Jesus' last days as a political revolt which ended in catastrophe, but he did not. If he had, it wouldn't matter to us. We know Jesus was not meant to sit on an earthly throne, some head of state calling the shots for humankind. Jesus is a greater ruler than that. He is true God. He knew how to save the world. And all who believe in him participate in his victory over evil and death.

Jesus knew how to live and how to die. He was a person of decision. He chose the cross over the crown. He became the lamb of God, a ransom for all of us. He met conflict with courage. He kept the communication lines open to the Father. He prepared to die. Because of his purposeful death, we have life forever and ever. Jesus is our true God!

---

1. "Now The Day Is Over," *Lutheran Book Of Worship*, Hymn 280, text: Sabine Baring-Gould, 1834-1924, alt.

Questions For Discussion

1) How did Jesus prepare to die?

2) What is involved in decision-making?

3) What turned off the Galileans?

4) What was the reaction of the disciples to Jesus' decision to go to Jerusalem?

5) Was Calvary an answer to prayer?

6) How much time should a believer spend in prayer?

6. Ministry Midst Determination

Scripture Reading: Matthew 21:1-11

Prayer: Let us talk with God:
O God, we confess our infidelity to Christ. Like ancient Jerusalem, we have often welcomed him with outward loyalty but before the week ends have crucified him. Grant us a fresh vision of his way of living, a resolute decision to let him be our Master, and a new willingness daily to take up our cross and follow him. Amen.

† † †

In 1937 on a gray, rainy day, I stood on Pennsylvania Avenue in Washington, D.C., waiting with thousands of others for Franklin Delano Roosevelt to ride by on his inauguration day. A first glimpse of a president is an exciting event. My friends and I had traveled 500 miles to see the inauguration.

Soldiers preceded the President, some marching, some on horseback, some in a terrifying display of armed strength. Bands played, with drums beating in unison with ominous tones. Planes flew overhead. Policemen kept the crowd back. FBI men secretly surveyed the crowd, watching for would-be assassins. By this time my heart was pumping hard. I hardly noticed the rain and the cold.

Then came the President in his open car, closely guarded by motorcycle policemen and secret service agents, dressed in his Prince Albert coat and waving his big top hat. It seemed he looked right at me and said, "Hello, Dale, my boy!"

In a moment it was all over. But that moment lives in my memory. It impressed me with the dignity and importance of the office of President. When I returned to school I told my friends: "I saw the President of the United States and he looked right at me!"

Jesus Christ made his last journey from Bethany to Jerusalem, no farther than from the Capitol to the White House — less than an hour's walk. Suppose you had been in that crowd which greeted him on that occasion which we call Palm Sunday? What would have been in your heart that day? Come with me and stand along the roadside as Jesus makes his journey to Jerusalem and certain death.

As we stand there in the hot sun on a Sunday morning, we hear others around us talk about Jesus of Nazareth.[1] "Back in Jericho, he restored the vision of a blind beggar named Bartimaeus," someone says. "I heard He raised Lazarus from the dead," shouts another, making himself heard above the excited crowd. "I wonder if Bartimaeus and Lazarus will be with him today," queries still another. Then one incident after another is related as people recall his preaching and teaching, his uncanny ability to look you in the eye and read your thoughts, plus his miracles of healing.

So our eyes look longingly toward Bethany in anticipation. We have heard He stopped at the home of Mary, Martha, and Lazarus in Bethany only last Friday. A big crowd had followed him the last twenty miles. Over the sabbath, of course, He could not travel. But today, Sunday, He will surely come to Jerusalem, as He promised.

The conversation around us now speculates on what Jesus will do when He arrives. A husky-voiced man makes his feelings known: "He should make history today. No prophet has had such a following as He. I expect him to proclaim himself our king. I for one will support him." "Me, too," a little man speaks up. A weak voice tries to be heard, "I hope He will have time to cure my cancer." Another says, "Or, bring my wife back to life. She rests over there in that cemetery," as he points across the road.

"There He comes!" everybody begins to shout. "Can you see him yet?" a little boy cries out, pulling at his mother's side. "Quick, pull a palm branch off that tree over there. Let's spread branches before him on the roadway as we do for returning conquering heroes. Wave to him as He goes by. He is our king!"

As Jesus comes closer we join with others shouting, "Hosanna in the highest!" O, how our hearts pound! This is Jesus of Nazareth, the healer, the miracle worker, the prophet and teacher. "Hallow this day, O God, in our hearts. The Messiah promised to deliver us has come! Children, this is the day our fathers prophesied would come!"

"Isn't that a cute colt He rides," a little girl is heard to say in a giggly voice. "There is Peter, the big fisherman. Look, there are James and John, Philip and Andrew, and Judas with the common purse, and all his disciples," the people point out. "Ride on, O Jesus, in majesty!"

Now swing your Lenten camera around. Focus the scene as from the eyes of Jesus Christ.

Jerusalem! On the way from Bethany his eyes can see the holy city with the Temple courts in plain view. He doesn't take the steep path. The other road, more roundabout but more comfortable, sweeps over the Mount of Olives, crosses the Kidron Valley by a bridge, and then ascends the slope which leads into the city gate. When He draws near, He weeps: "If you, even you, had only recognized on this day the things that make for peace! But now they are hidden from your eyes. Indeed, the days will come upon you, when your enemies will set up ramparts around you and surround you, and hem you in on every side. They will crush you to the ground, you and your children within you, and they will not leave within you one stone upon another; because you did not recognize the time of your visitation from God" (Luke 19:42-44).

As Jesus rides the colt into the city, He can see the thousands upon thousands of people lined along the way. The great Feast of the Passover has brought up to three million people into the area. They have come from overseas, from Asia Minor and Egypt, from wherever a Jewish ear has been trained in the law of Moses.

What does Jesus see as He rides along? He can see that some have come to Jerusalem because of a deep religious heritage. They have come to observe a solemn festival heralding freedom from slavery. He can also see that some come primarily to renew friendships and to enjoy family reunions. He can see that others come for business reasons, hoping to profit by the festival event.

He can see the religious authorities standing in amazement at the crowd's apparent stupidity and hoping Jesus will make some religious blunder or political slip that will enable them to kill him.

Jesus can see that some have come to see him. In the crowd are thousands from the south who had recently heard him preach. There are some Galileans who still have hope for him. And there are thousands of others who have heard of him but have never seen him.

Jesus knows why He has come. This was no uncertain journey. He has come to die! Turning His head, Jesus can see and hear the multitude of disciples rejoicing and praising God for all the mighty works they had seen. Now, they feel, his hour has come and this demonstration is more the way they have envisioned his ministry. "Blessed is the king who comes in the name of the Lord! Peace in heaven, and glory in the highest heaven!" (Luke 19:38). The Pharisees don't like that. They ask Jesus to quiet his disciples. Jesus replies, "I tell you, if these were silent, the stones would shout out" (Luke 19:40).

Entering the city, Jesus cannot help noticing the Jerusalemites. They have no part in his "triumphal" journey. They have to ask strangers what all the noise is about and just who He is.

Getting down off the colt, Jesus could have been remembering the Temple when it was being defiled and how He drove out the marketeers with strong words and stronger action, "It is written, 'My house shall be a house of prayer'; but you have made it a den of robbers" (Luke 19:46).

The Pharisees and scribes are now leagued together. They select their most learned people to come up with a question which will seal the doom of this upstart from Nazareth. They are slick with false praise. They ask Jesus: "Teacher, we know that you are right in what you say and teach, and you show deference to no one, but teach the way of God in accordance with truth. Is it lawful for us to pay taxes to the emperor, or not?" Jesus is quick with a reply. " 'Show me a denarius. Whose head and whose title does it bear?' They said, 'The emperor's.' He said to them, 'Then give to the emperor the things that are the emperor's, and to God the things that are God's' " (Luke 20:24-25). They are stunned. They do not know what to say. They had not anticipated that He could answer.

Jesus can see within the eyes of the people that this was the time they anticipated his announcement of kingship. He can see it on their faces and in their hearts. Their economic and political hopes have shrunk their spiritual capacity. Abruptly, He withdraws and goes back to Bethany, and as He walks alone He can see the deep disappointment in their eyes. By refusing to proclaim himself king, He has in effect humiliated the people in the presence of the scribes and Pharisees. He has insulted them. The stage is set for the certain journey to the cross. He cannot win the people by appeasement and acquiescence. He can only die for them. He can only bestow faith. He can free them from their sin.

It is not likely that in Holy Week we will cry, "Crucify him! Crucify him!" We may be spending our time figuring out how much silver we can accumulate before another economic crunch descends. We may be occupied with other things, too busy to fit into our schedules a couple nights to worship. Furthermore, we are more likely to settle for a facsimile of faith.

Theologians know that the Antichrist does not announce his antagonism toward Christ today. If the Antichrist did, his capacity for destroying our faith in the Savior would be slight. No, the great danger of Antichrist is that he so closely counterfeits Christ, so skillfully impersonates His spirit, so exactly forges promises that seem Christlike, so cleverly appears to be Christian. Even good people can be deceived because the mask is so lifelike. It is through superficial similarities that profound deception does its work.

When you see Jesus Christ this week, don't just wave to him from the street. Go up and shake his cross — the real test of his humanity. Go up and look into his empty tomb — the real test of his divinity.

Admire all you want a president of the United States, but don't mistake democracy for Christianity. Study other religions all you want, but don't let a mask trick you into thinking it is the Master.

This Savior-God of ours is bound for glory this week. On a little colt He comes. No army will be in sight. There will be no brass band. There will be only organ music and choirs singing, believers praying and rejoicing, people kneeling in thankfulness that God came in Christ and reconciled the world unto himself. Tell that to the stock market! Tell that to people who are consumed with their personal existence! Tell that to people who live in an affluent age and are afraid! Tell everyone that Jesus Christ is true God!

It is great to hear a crowd roar, especially at some athletic extravaganza like the Olympics. God is more pleased with individuals and congregations who confess, "We believe in one Lord, Jesus Christ ... begotten, not made ... (who) for us and our salvation ... came down from heaven ... and was made man ... was crucified ... and rose again in accordance with the Scriptures ... and his kingdom will have no end...."[2]

---

1. See Mark 10:46-52.

2. The Nicene Creed

Questions For Discussion

1) From Jesus' point of view — was Palm Sunday a success or not?

2) Who welcomed Jesus into Jerusalem?

3) What was the trick question asked of Jesus and how did He handle it?

4) What is meant by Antichrist?

5) Do you believe there is a devil? If so, why?

6) Do we wrestle with the devil today? Give an example.

7. Ministry Midst Death

Scripture Reading: Exodus 12:1-14; John 13:1-36

Prayer: Let us talk with God:
O God, we have difficulty discerning all the implications of Jesus' gift of his life. At times we question the need for sacrifice. Give us a new and deeper understanding of who you are and who we are. In Jesus' name. Amen.

† † †

Every male Hebrew thirteen years and older who was able to travel to Jerusalem for the Passover was there. The highways had been clogged and ships from Asia Minor and Egypt had carried pilgrims to this greatest religious observance of the year — the Passover. Two to three million people had descended upon Jerusalem. As a precautionary measure, because of the crowds, Pilate found it necessary to travel to Jerusalem from Caesarea to preserve law and order.

It is critical for our understanding of Jesus' last days to recall the historical background of the Passover. The book of Exodus provides information.

In the second half of the second millennium before Christ the Israelites had been slaves of the Egyptians for 430 years. God called Moses to act as God's agent in letting the people go free. Moses received specific instruction from God about how to accomplish this, inflicting a plague upon the people of Egypt every time the Pharaoh refused to let the Israelites go. The plagues included water turned to blood, frogs, gnats, flies, diseased livestock, boils, thunder and hail, locusts, and darkness. When a plague occurred, the Pharaoh promised Moses he would let the Israelites go if he would rid Egypt of the plague. Nine times after a plague disappeared, the Pharaoh reneged.

Finally, God instructed Moses to tell the Israelites to slay a sacrificial lamb and to pour the blood of the animal over the doorposts of their homes. Animal sacrifice was a part of their Hebrew religion. God told Moses that an angel would pass over the homes during the night. In the homes that did not display this sign of belief in God, the firstborn son would be slain. As a consequence, Egyptian homes suffered the loss of their firstborn, even in the court of the Pharaoh. It was then the Egyptians pleaded with the Pharaoh to get rid of these people. The Pharaoh told Moses to take his people and go. Ever since that time, Jews have observed the "Passover" — when the angel of God passed over their homes and triggered their freedom.

When Jesus set his face toward Jerusalem for the certain journey to death, it was to observe the Passover with his disciples. The Passover was now a major religious festival heralding Israelite freedom, something like Americans celebrating the Fourth of July. At first, the Passover date was selected according to agricultural seasons. Later it was designated as a 24-hour period beginning at sundown on the fourteenth day of Nisan, the first month of the Hebrew year, late March or early April (Leviticus 23:5). Then it was linked to the Feast of the Unleavened Bread, which derived from Semitic shepherds observing a feast of sacrifice and farmers paying tribute to the deities of their fields, in the spring of the year (Exodus 5:1-3). Thus, the Passover season became eight days, including the 24-hour day of the actual Passover.

The ritual of the Passover included the sacrifice of paschal lambs slain in various sections of Jerusalem and taken to the priests, who offered sacrifical portions to God at the altar. The remaining portions of the lambs were taken to homes, where no fewer than ten men and usually no more than twenty ate one animal. In those days only the men were counted. Bitter herbs were eaten, reminding them of the bitterness of Egyptian slavery. Unleavened cakes were dipped in sweet sauce and eaten, reminding them of the haste of departure. Four cups of wine were drunk. The father of the home would bless the first cup and pass it around. The eldest son would describe the meaning of the feast. The Hallel (Psalms 113, 114) was sung. The second cup was passed around and the meal eaten. The third cup was blessed, with a prayer of thanksgiving. While the fourth cup was passed, Psalms 115-118 were sung. This is what Jesus and His disciples would do. I would have loved to hear Jesus and the disciples sing, wouldn't you? Some people in church do not sing. They ought to follow Jesus' example.

After the triumphal entry into Jerusalem, Jesus returned to Bethany, the home of Mary, Martha, and Lazarus. During the week Jesus went to the Temple in Jerusalem and engaged in teaching and healing. Now the Pharisees, Sadducees, Herodians, priests and scribes were convinced Jesus was a deceptor and a threat to orthodoxy, and should be eliminated. They combined their efforts in this common cause. They came to him at the Temple and demanded of him by what authority He ministered. With all the pomp of officialdom, they set themselves against the Galilean in full view of the multitude. They entered into prolonged controversy, endeavoring to trick him in debate. In an orchestrated way, their champions challenged Christ. But they were no match for him. He met their attacks with cogent answers. There is vivid discourse: "Woe to you, scribes and Pharisees, hypocrites! For you are like whitewashed tombs, which on the outside look beautiful, but inside they are full of the bones of the dead and of all kinds of filth. So you also on the outside look righteous to others, but inside you are full of hypocrisy and lawlessness" (Matthew 23:27-28). Jesus was known to be gentle and kind. He also could call a "spade a spade"!

Church leaders today don't talk like that, do they? If they talked like Jesus, they wouldn't last long. After all, we want harmony in the Church. Bishops spend much of their time in the area of promoting peace. We avoid stress at all times, sometimes at the cost of truth. The question persists, however, prompted by Jesus. Have you or I whitewashed Christianity? The question makes me quiver.

The cross is in sight now. Yet Jesus is not consumed by that thought. His thoughts are for the disciples. At a time when He could very well have been preoccupied with the events yet to take place and what would happen to him, He thinks of others. Love is like that. Translators have helped us to understand the intensity of the situation by translating John 13:1 in these words: "He loved them unto the uttermost." His love extended to the absolute ultimate limit. "He loved them to the end."

I have read that the sun pours out its rays and if it is not continually replenished would ultimately cease to shine and would be a dead, cold mass of ashes. Not so with the Son of Humankind who endures forever. He pours out his love and there is no bankruptcy by this expenditure, no exhaustion of his love, no diminution of his store of mercy. As the psalmist phrases it, "Your steadfast love, O Lord, endures forever" (Psalm 138:8). Jesus came to save humankind.

On what we call "Maundy" (command) Thursday, Jesus prepared for the last supper with his disciples. When the disciples arrived at that upper room, their feet were dirty, for they had walked the unpaved and unclean streets of Jerusalem. A servant usually washed the feet of weary travelers. Christ took the place of a servant. He washed the disciples' feet.

It was Peter who protested Jesus' act of washing the disciples' feet. He and the other disciples had been too proud to wash one another's feet. But in this humbling example of Christ, Peter and the other disciples learned that "all who exalt themselves will be humbled, and all who humble themselves will be exalted" (Matthew 23:12).

Love is like that. An outstanding television commercial some time ago pictured a little boy offering a Coke to "Mean" Joe Greene, the professional football player, as he walked from the playing field through a tunnel, and Joe giving the boy the shirt off his back as a remembrance. Both were acts of love.

But there is more here than a person's heart touched by a gesture. Genuine love is more than a gesture, over in a moment. Love is a gift that lasts forever. Christ loved them to the "uttermost." He didn't hold anything back. The gospel writers, Matthew, Mark, and Luke, are concerned with details as they portray the last supper. The Gospel of John is more concerned about the attitude of Christ with his disciples. Both emphases are important. In the supper, Christ makes animal sacrifice obsolete as He gives himself as the paschal lamb. He gives himself so that believers yet to come can experience his coming into their lives "in, with, and under" the elements, as Luther describes. We, too, come to the supper dirty. We need cleansing. Forgiveness of sin comes from the Savior of the world, true God. Nothing is held back.

Christ's example at this supper and during the coming night is an inspiration to every believer. He teaches us about pride. We can betray him, as Judas did. We can deny him, as Peter did. We can argue among ourselves about how Christian we are. But the place of every believer is on the knees saying, "God, be merciful to me, a sinner!" (Luke 18:13). Thanks be to God for that mercy. Only Christ, true God, can bestow mercy and save us from our sins.

The hour was fast approaching for Jesus to be crucified. Yet, at this hour, these uncomprehending disciples argue about who is to have chief place at the table with him. As was custom in those days at a Jewish feast, the table was in the form of a square with one end open. The host sat at the center. The honored guests sat closest to the host, beginning to the right and then to the left.

There at the table sits a person who is to betray him. There sits another who will deny he ever knew him. There sit others who will not even show up at the crucifixion. And yet, they all have a special place in the heart of Christ. Christ understood their humanity. They were to learn of his divinity. These disciples experienced a closeness to Christ that Maundy night as He instituted the last supper and gave commands to eat and drink of him. But the night was to get darker as they made their way to the Garden of Gethsemane for prayer. "Night brings out the stars," my mother used to say. In the darkness of that Garden there is the light of Christ's prayers. He submits to the will of the Father. He experiences disappointment upon finding time and again the disciples fast asleep.

As I stood in the Garden of Gethsemane, I noticed a cat asleep under an olive tree. The disciples were like that cat — they could not fight away sleep. The betrayer made his way, accompanied by soldiers of authority, and bestowed an identifying kiss. They led him away. They put Christ on trial. He didn't even defend himself. They mocked him. Outside the city wall they nailed our Lord to a cross as a common criminal, between two criminals.

When you go to that place today, supposedly the place where the crucifixion took place, there is a business establishment across the street. It was symbolic for me as I stared in one direction envisioning three crosses, and across the street merchants were scurrying around, business as usual. Little did the world know then what they were doing. Countless people today still miss the Savior of the world in the pursuit of a livelihood. Yet, the stars do shine. They turn into a radiant dawn.

Christ "... came to what was his own, and his own people did not accept him. But to all who received him, who believed in his name, he gave power to become children of God, who were born, not of blood or of the will of the flesh or of the will of man, but of God" (John 1:11-13).

The late Rufus Jones of Haverford College lost his little son, Lowell, at the age of eleven. He wrote these words:

"When my sorrow was at its most acute stage, I was walking along a great city highway. Suddenly I saw a little child come out of a great gate, which swung to and fastened behind her. She wanted to go back into her home behind the gate, but it would not open. She pounded in vain with her little fists. She rattled the gate. She wailed as if her heart would break. The cry brought the mother. She caught the child in her arms and kissed away the tears. 'Didn't you know I would come? It is all right now.' All of a sudden, I saw with my spirit that there was love behind my shut gate. When there is so much love, there must be more."

What Jesus is saying to us in his life on earth is simply, "Didn't you know I would come? It is all right now." "When there is so much love, there must be more."

Questions For Discussion

1) What was the Exodus? When did it occur?

2) Detail the Passover Feast.

3) Did the disciples sing? Did Jesus sing? Was He a tenor or a bass? Is it important for worshipers to sing? Why?

4) Have we whitewashed Christianity?

5) Did Jesus oppose anybody? Should we?

6) Why don't we wash one another's feet?

7) Was the cross necessary? Why?

8. Fulfillment Of Prophecy

Scripture Reading: John 1:1-18

Prayer: Let us talk with God:
O God, we pray for those who feel defeated and who cannot imagine victory because it sounds distant and unreal. You see them among us, known to you but not to us, whose spirits are frustrated by circumstance, overwhelmed by temptation, facing griefs too heavy for their solitary strength. O Risen Lord, who can make the barren place rejoice and the desert to bloom, redeem some stricken soul here from defeat to victory. Amen.

† † †

When the sun went down on Easter eve, there was peace of mind for the religious authorities and the politically-minded Romans. They had combined their authority and were successful in putting Christ to death. The day before, Jesus of Nazareth, the miracle worker and itinerant preacher, was nailed to a cross and died. Death is final. The body soon becomes lifeless and cold as a stone.

Romans were proficient in carrying out crucifixions. They had a lot of experience in capital punishment. They made certain of his death by ordering a soldier to stick a spear in his side.

The religious authorities did not leave anything to chance, either. The priests and Pharisees met with Pilate and said, "Sir, we remember what that impostor said while he was still alive, 'After three days I will rise again.' Therefore command the tomb to be made secure until the third day; otherwise his disciples may go and steal him away, and tell the people, 'He has been raised from the dead,' and the last deception would be worse than the first" (Matthew 27:63-64).

The disciples, however, were in no mood for deception. Those who feel they have been deceived are not likely to manufacture a story on behalf of the person who apparently deceived them. The disciples had had enough! The upper room was an exciting experience with the supper and all. But, Gethsemane broke their hearts. When the soldiers took Jesus by force, the disciples thought He should have fought back. Certainly Peter thought so, as he tried to fight with a sword. Where did he get the sword? Did he grab it from a soldier? Did he and the other disciples still think that Jesus would proclaim himself king? The trial that followed disillusioned them. Christ, ever so docile, did not even defend himself. Then the crucifixion! They were so far from the cross they would have had to have a telescopic lens to see it. Whatever they saw made them sick. Manufacture a story about the resurrection? Ha! They were stunned, subdued, and defeated. The big fisherman denied knowing him. Poor Judas hanged himself. "I didn't see any of the others, did you? Except John at the cross, but he is a meek individual. I hear he took the deceiver's mother home with him."

Conversation around the Temple on the sabbath, the day after the crucifixion, must have sounded like our Friendship Time after church. The Passover Festival was celebrated as usual. The priests performed their rites. Victory was sweet. No longer would they have to hear stories about the miracle worker. Even Pilate, no longer troubled by his wife's warnings, could lie down in his palace and relax. Not only had he washed his hands of the whole affair, his province was over a crisis. His position was still secure.

We like to recall a victory and savor the experience. The priests must have remembered Jesus on the cross and how they made him eat his words: "He saved others; he cannot save himself" (Matthew 27:42).

The soldiers must have remembered the fun they had with Jesus. They stripped him. They spit on him. They knelt before him and mocked him by offering him a crown of thorns while twisting the crown on his head. They laughingly joked, "Hail, King of the Jews!"

Good Friday was good for them. The sabbath Saturday was sweet in memory. No disciples of the deceiver had claimed his body. They didn't seem to mind that rich fellow, Joseph from Arimathea, asking Pilate for the body. They didn't even mind Nicodemus preparing his body for burial according to Jewish tradition. It was all over. Death is final. And with the grave sealed and armed soldiers guarding it, the religious authorities and the Romans had peace of mind.

Peace of mind is no guarantee of godliness. It can seal the mind, making it immune to revealed truth. It can guard the entrance to the human heart, making it cold and unreceptive. Even religious leaders, like the Pharisees and scribes, can be misled by conscience and derailed by pride. We run that danger, too. We can attempt to explain everything about God and leave no room for faith.

Never shall I forget a plane ride going into Santiago, Chile, some years ago. It was in the days when smoking was permitted anywhere in the cabin. A man sitting next to me spoke as he watched the smoke from his cigarette curl into a ring: "The resurrection of Jesus Christ from the dead is an unreasonable claim. The Bible is a collection of writings whose man-made original manuscripts have been lost forever. I cannot believe the scriptures as the word of God any more than I can accept your words reported by another. And, I have peace of mind when I say that."

This man left no room in his life for faith. He was filled up with himself and fed up with religion. Like Bethlehem with "no room in the inn," there was no space in his life for Christ, as we descended to the ground surrounded by the beauty of God's creation.

Disbelievers will not always have peace of mind. Evil will not always win. There is the prophecy, "And on the third day he will be raised" (Matthew 20:19).

There was no peace of mind, of course, for the disciples. Death had struck twice among them on the same day — Jesus on the cross and Judas on a tree. Denial had played havoc with their seared consciences. Second-guessing must have been a favorite pastime, "If only I had ..." and the words trailed off into silence. Death and denial and disillusionment had brought them together. There is no comfort in being alone when catastrophe hits. We need to be with others at the time of death. There is strength in combined comfort. The little unborn Church did not have much to say. The disciples didn't even go to the grave. It was the women who took the spices to the tomb to care for the body of Jesus.

When Jesus was born, angels sang to shepherds. When Jesus came to life in a cemetery, it was an angel who made the announcement: "Do not be alarmed; you are looking for Jesus of Nazareth, who was crucified. He has been raised; he is not here. Look, there is the place they laid him. But go, tell his disciples and Peter that he is going ahead of you to Galilee; there you will see him, just as he told you" (Mark 16:6-7).

Prophecy fulfilled! In these few sentences of the angel, our hearts tremble. So must have the hearts of the disciples! John didn't jog but ran to the tomb and had a look at the linen cloths. Peter went into the tomb and bent over the cloth that had been on Jesus' head. It was neatly folded. Carefully Peter handled it.

You and I can only handle the Scriptures. But like Peter and John we can leave room for faith! We can bend the knee in belief! We can go home today and not wonder what happened after the crucifixion.

For Mary from Magdala, Jesus' resurrection was answer to her tears and sobbing voice as she cried, "They have taken away my Lord and I do not know where they have laid him." Then with Mary we exclaim, "Rabboni!" (John 20:13, 16). The disciples did not believe Mary when she told them that Christ was alive. While the disciples hid behind locked doors, still afraid of the religious authorities, Christ entered and spoke, "Peace be with you" (John 20:19). He scolded them because their minds were closed and did not believe those who had seen him.

We cannot go into a cemetery and see Jesus, but we can go into his church and worship him, and receive him in the last supper. We cannot expect Christ to walk through the wall in full view of worshipers, but we can hear him say, "Blessed are those who have not seen and yet have come to believe" (John 20:29).

For the guards, the resurrection meant a pocketful of money. They were bribed by the high priests to say, "His disciples came by night and stole him away while we were asleep" (Matthew 28:13).

For the men on the way to Emmaus, the resurrection meant seven miles of walking with a stranger, hearing again the messianic prophecies of old beginning with Moses, before realizing the stranger was the Savior.

We cannot walk to Emmaus today, but our hearts can burn within us as God speaks through God's word. We cannot eat breakfast along the seashore with Jesus, but we can share the bread of life with all people.

Jesus Christ can roll away any stone. He can unlock any life and set a person free. This is what the risen Christ did for the disciples. He spoke to them, "Thus it is written, that the Messiah is to suffer and to rise from the dead on the third day, and that repentance and forgiveness of sins is to be proclaimed in his name to all nations, beginning from Jerusalem. You are witnesses of these things" (Luke 24:46-48).

For another forty days after the resurrection, Jesus opened the Scriptures to the disciples, preparing them to be on their own but not alone. His last words were to "go ... and make disciples of all nations" (Matthew 28:19). It was a command to the disciples and to every believer who would follow. Could He have meant for us today to make disciples not only of Caucasians, Africans, Mexicans, and Asians but of all immigrants who have come into our backyard recently?

For the disciples the resurrection meant God's victory over evil and death. It also meant that this Good News must be shared with all people everywhere. Each gave his life for this cause. There was no more uncertainty about the meaning and purpose of Christ's kingdom.

This is the life of Christ, made up of preparation for life and death, shuttled between popularity and prejudice, opposed but not oppressed, destined to take a certain journey to the cross, and finally fulfilling prophecy in the resurrection. He invites us to live as He lived!

What does Christ's life and the resurrection mean to you? This is what Scripture claims:

1) Evil will not finally win. We need to keep this truth in focus when tragedy occurs. The tragedies of life can be turned into triumphs. It may appear for a while that evil is in charge as we struggle with the inequities and uncertainties of our world. The resurrection, however, tells us that a few days can make a difference. Defeat today — Victory tomorrow! In Christ, there is always hope. God is the ultimate victor. Put your life on the side of good!

2) Death is not final. Death is not to be feared; it is to be faced. It can happen to anyone at any time, from the moment a baby squirms into life to the aged person worn out by life. Death is not all there is. A resurrected Christ assures us there is life beyond what the human eye can see. There is life beyond a tomb, beyond a rock. Because of the unfamiliarity with what is beyond, since none of us knows exactly what eternal life will be like, we tend to dread death's invitation. We see through a glass darkly. Our Lord reassures us that He will be with us in our coming and our going. He has won the victory over humankind's last enemy — death. He invites faith. Put your life on the side of Christ and receive faith!

3) Sacrifice is necessary. Before the resurrection there is a cross. What good is the shooting out of the lip without the sacrificing of the life? "Those who find their life will lose it, and those who lose their life for my sake will find it" (Matthew 10:39). There is no shortcut to eternity. Faith is a gift but there is a price to pay. There is no "cheap grace" as Bonhoeffer (the German pastor who was executed just before the second World War concluded) stated. If you evade active identity with the Christian cause, do not complain about how far away God seems. If you evade dealing with your pet sin, do not expect to get away with it. If you are always finding fault and you are a chronic complainer, do not expect joy and love to come into your life. The resurrection means giving every area of your life to God. When you and I do that, then we can tell it out abroad — this Good News that the Christ lives in our lives! Put your life on the side of Good News!

When you choose Christ, as your Lord over all, life and death and the assurance of eternal life, this true God comes into focus. If your Lenten camera is still rolling, you have come to know that nothing can thwart the love and power of Jesus Christ, Our Lord and true God.

Questions For Discussion

1) Why were the disciples disillusioned? Are we?

2) What gives peace of mind?

3) Do we need Easter proof?

4) What is meant by "repentance"? Is it necessary?

5) Is it necessary to believe that Jesus is God?

6) How do you react when death knocks on your family door?

7) Do you believe there is a heaven? A hell?

8) If you are a Christian, why are you a Christian?

www.ingramcontent.com/pod-product-compliance
Lightning Source LLC
Chambersburg PA
CBHW071744040426
42446CB00012B/2475